Architectural Design Coloring Book

Mark W. Bemish

ARCHITECTURAL DESIGN
COLORING BOOK

Coloring is FUN! I like to also doodle and then color or shade the drawings with colored pencils or markers. Once in a while I get the watercolors out. If you feel like adding things or people to the images – go ahead.

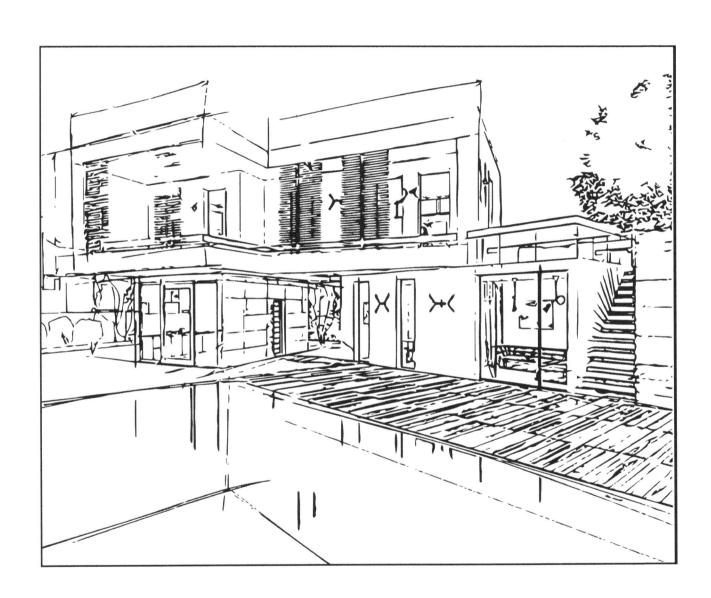

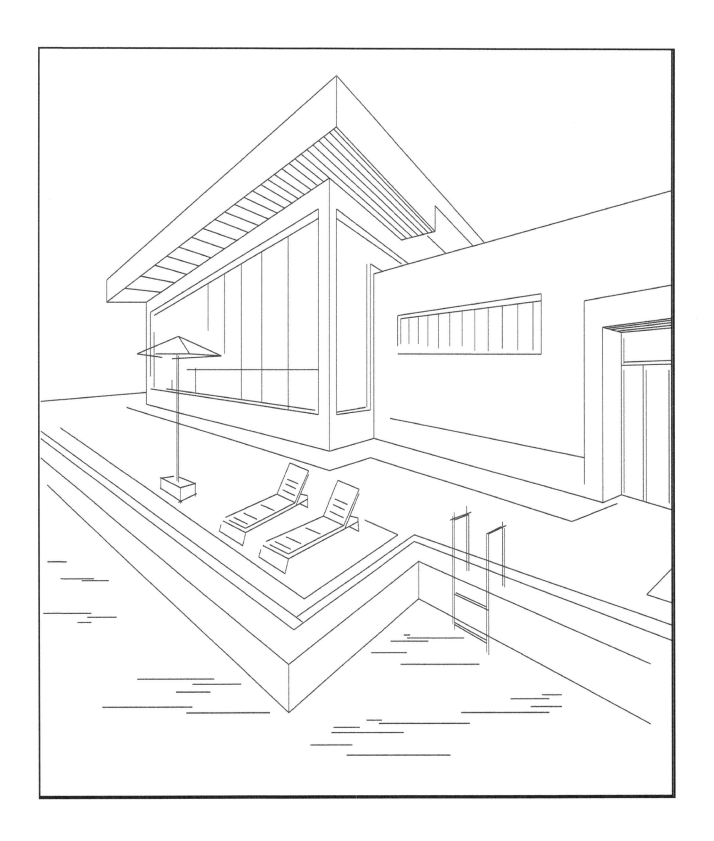

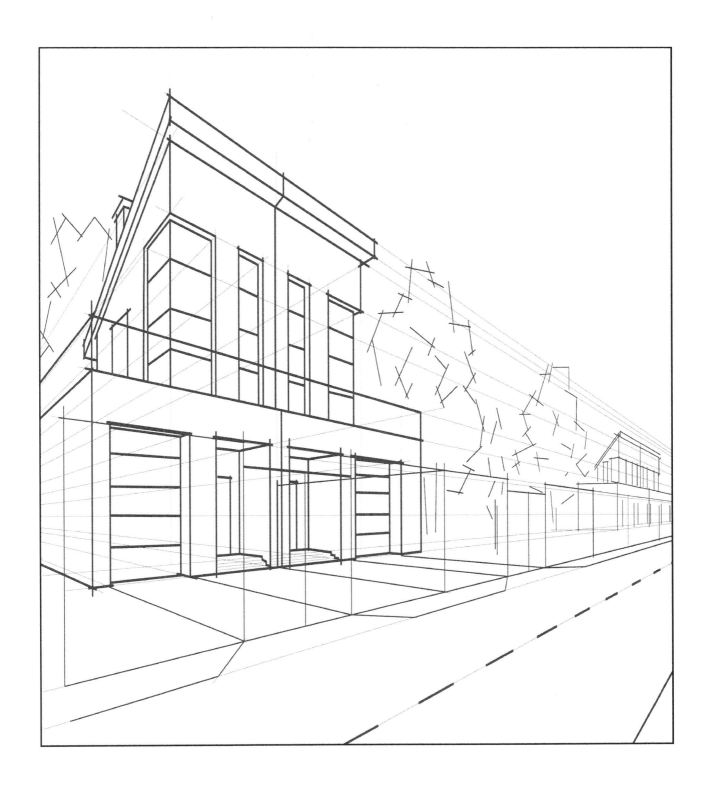

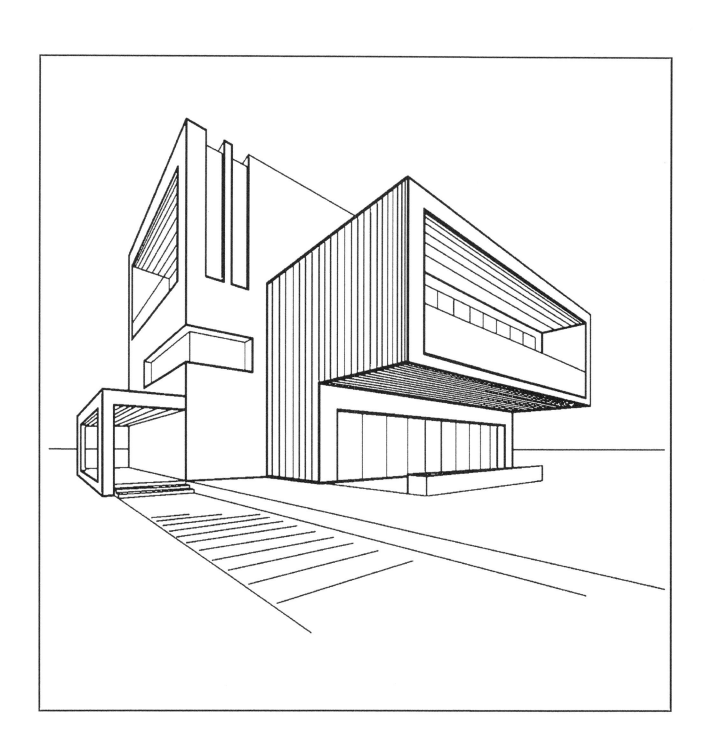

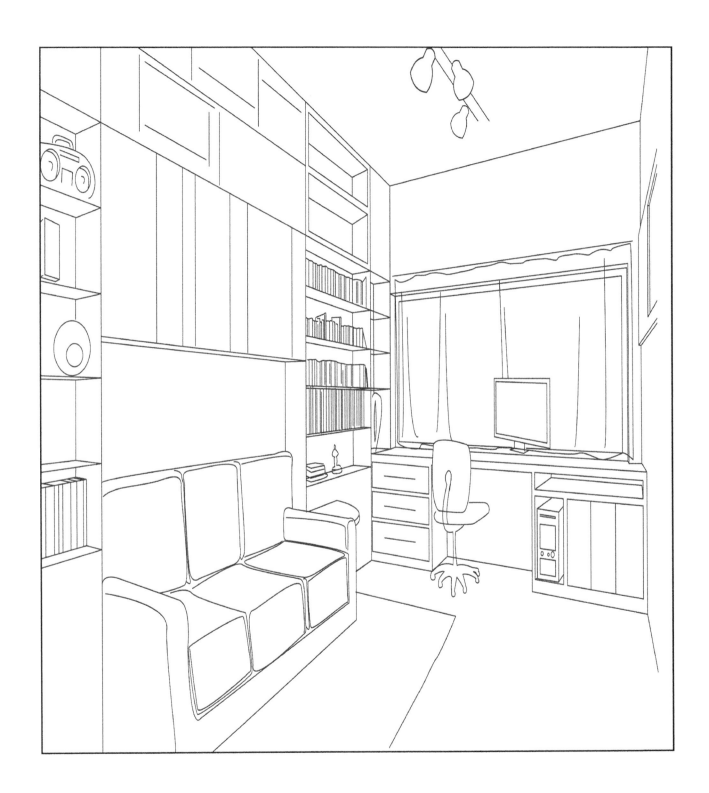

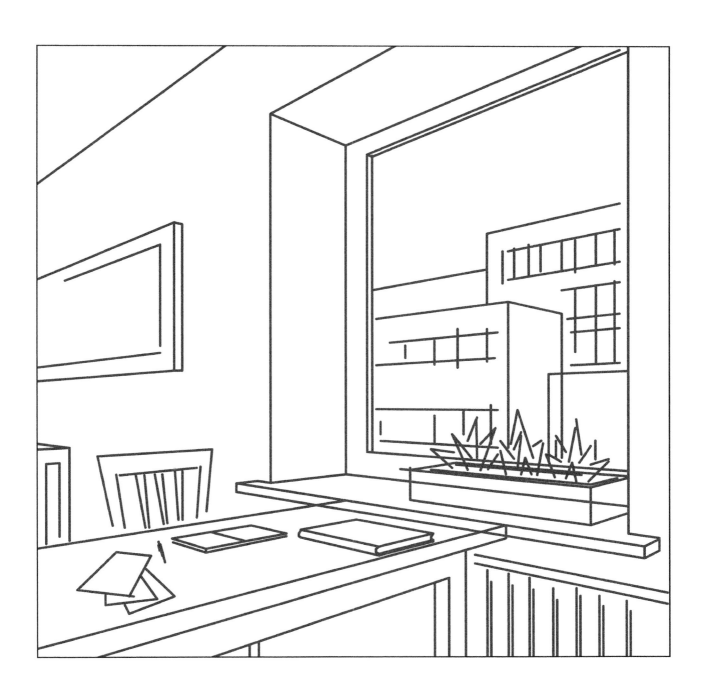

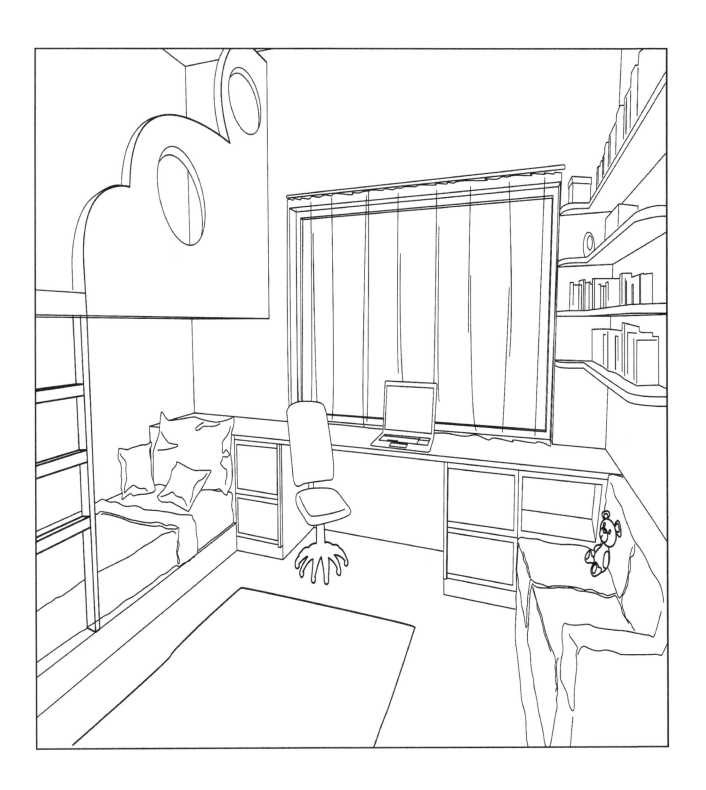

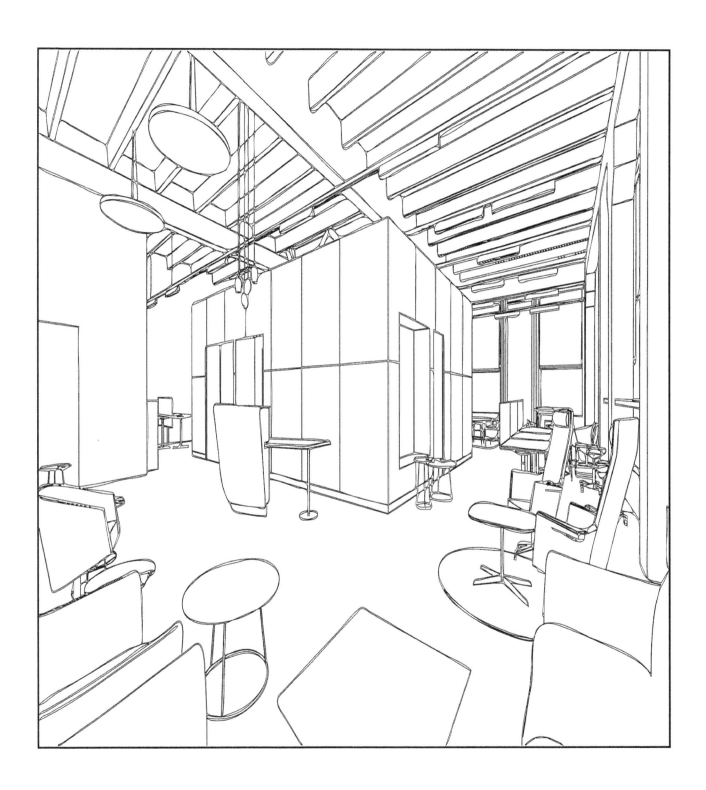

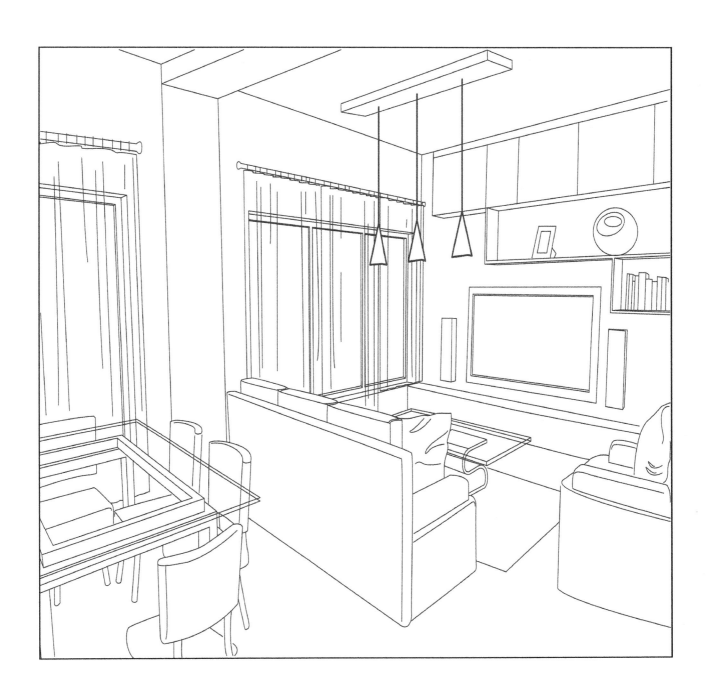

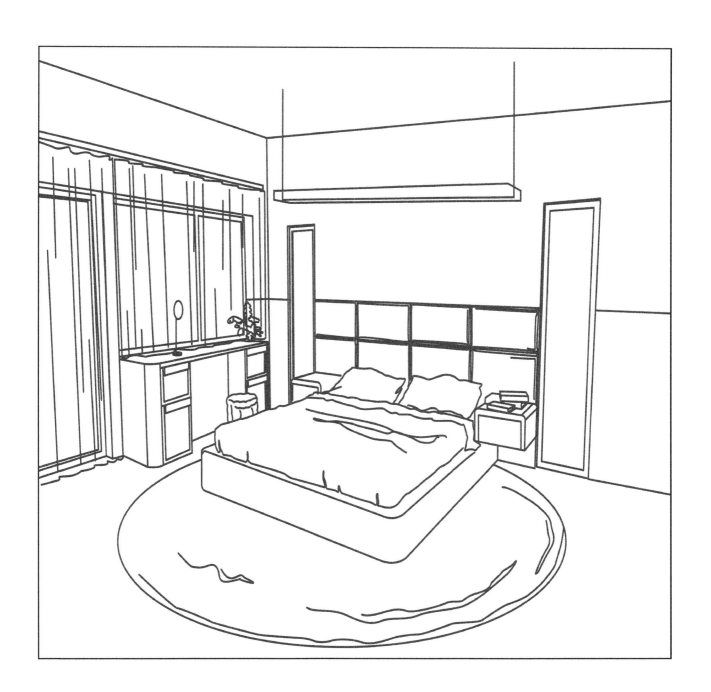

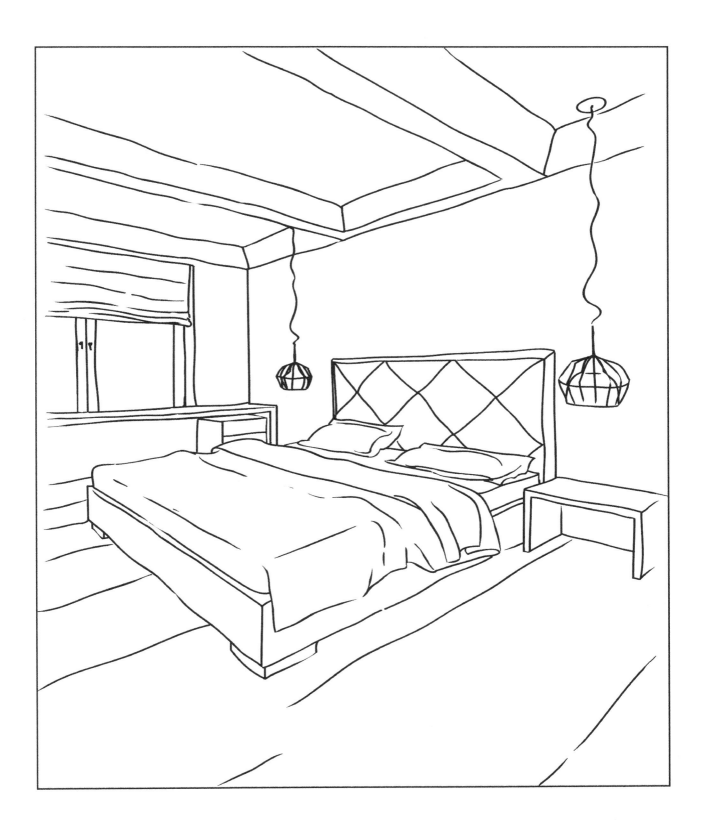

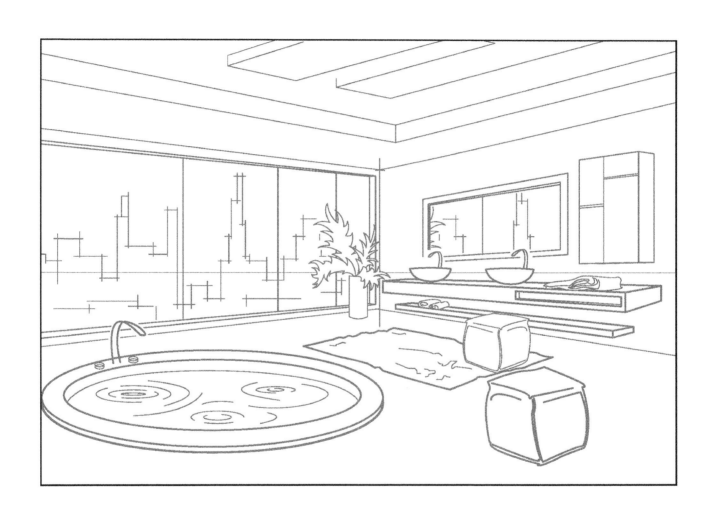

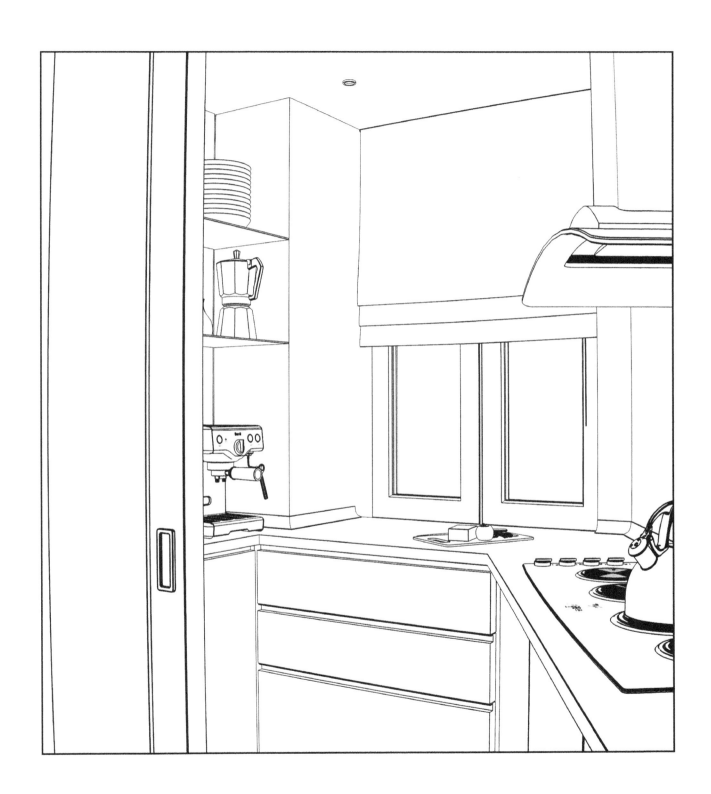

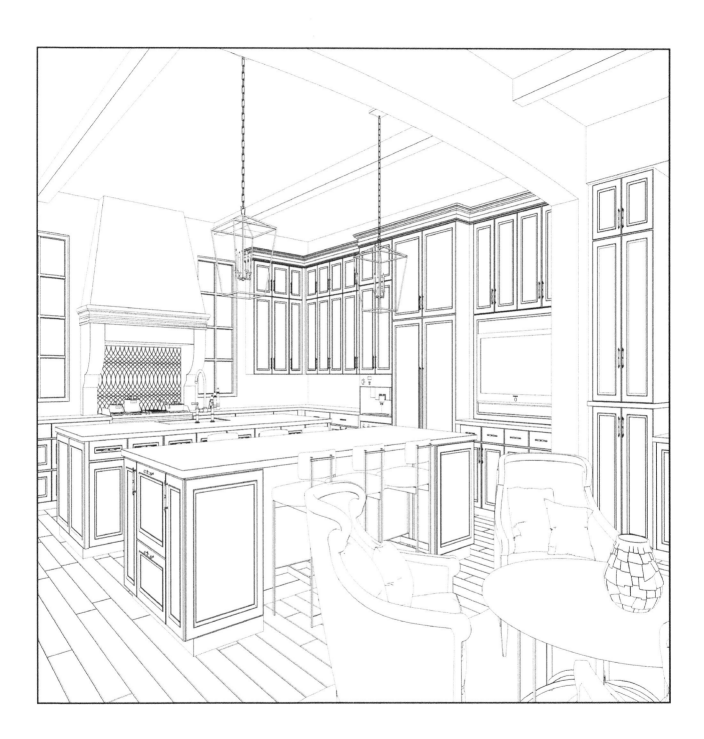

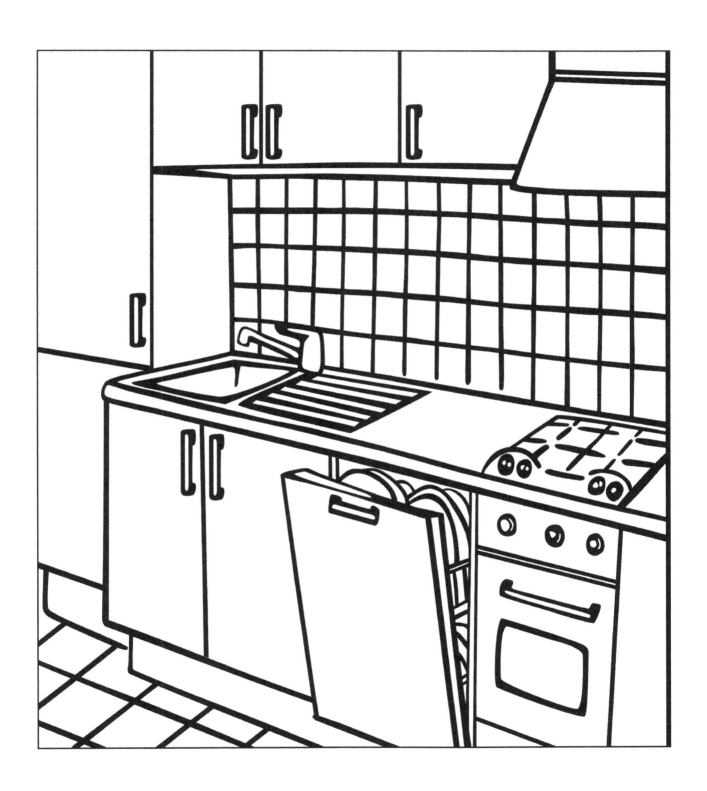

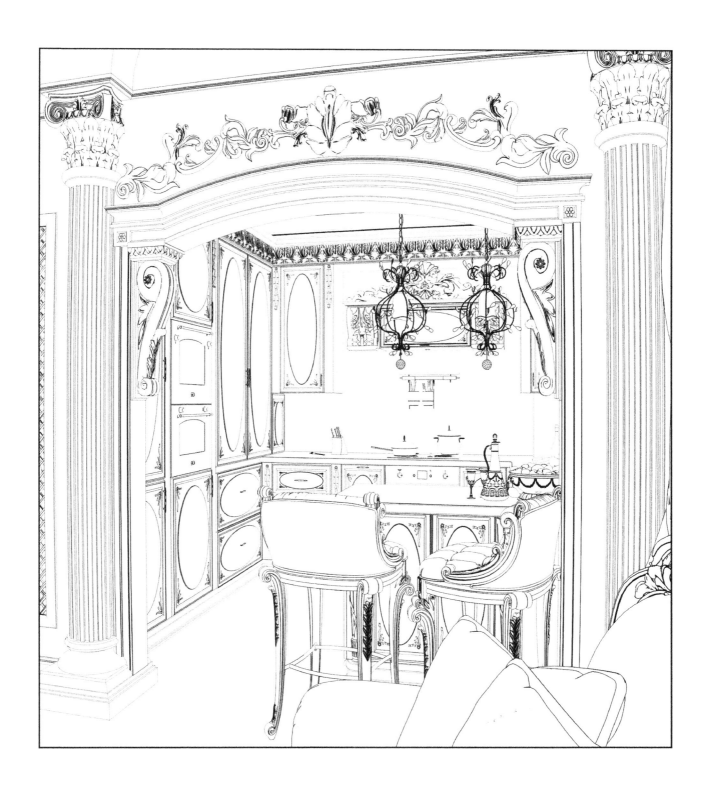

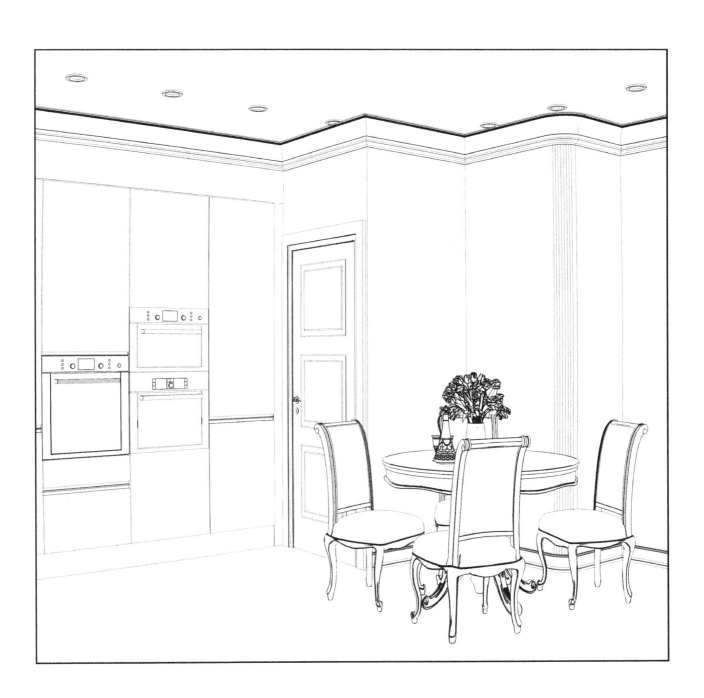

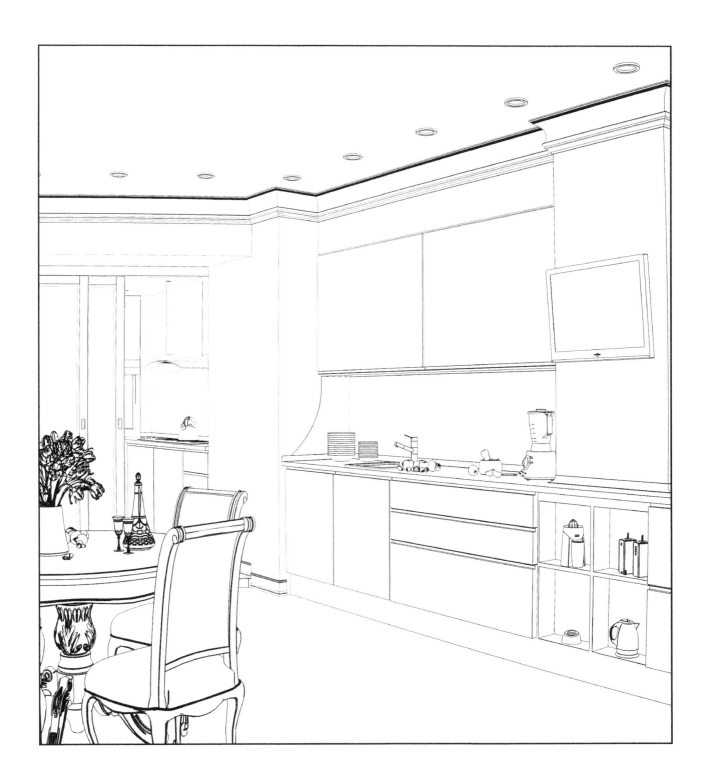

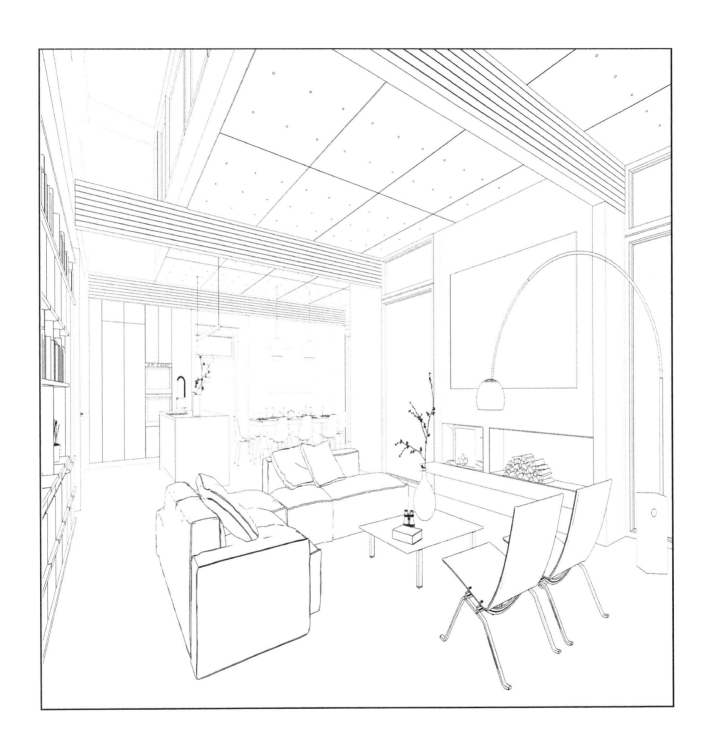

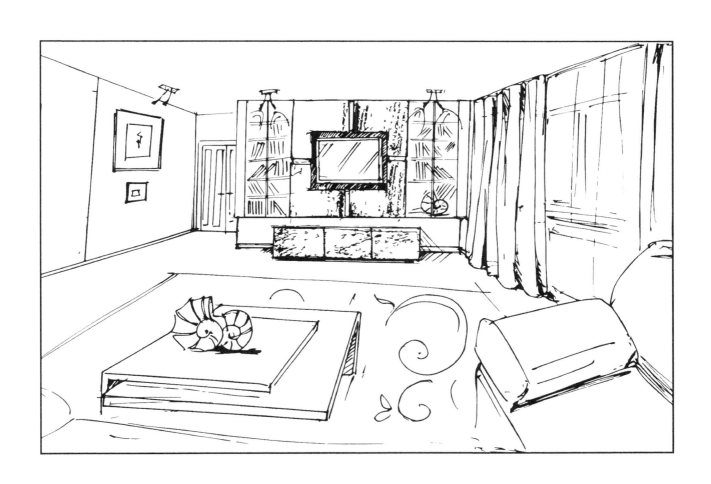

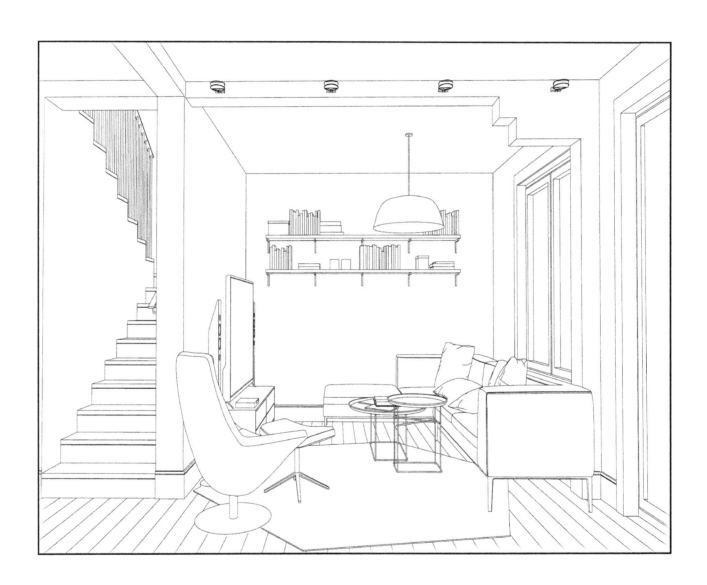

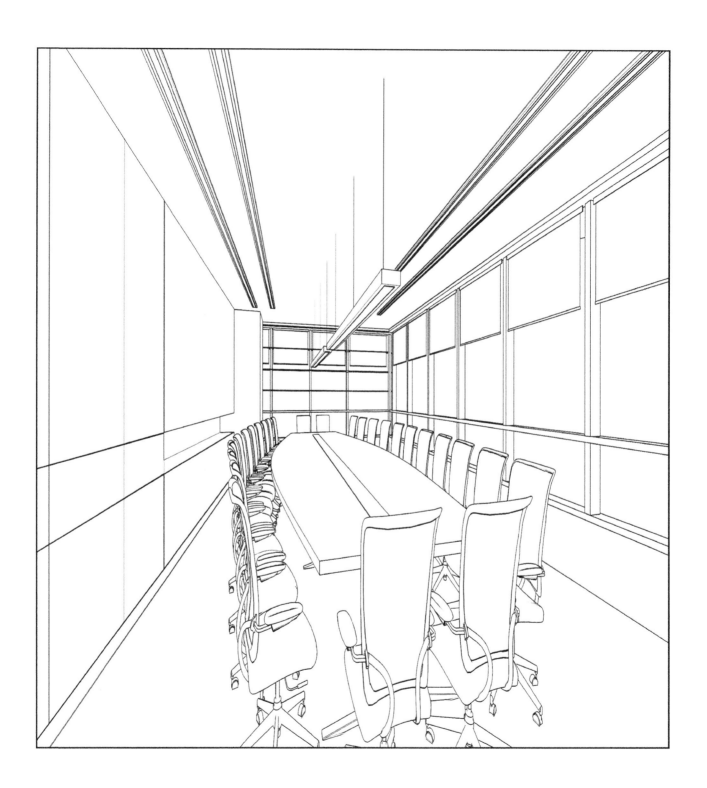

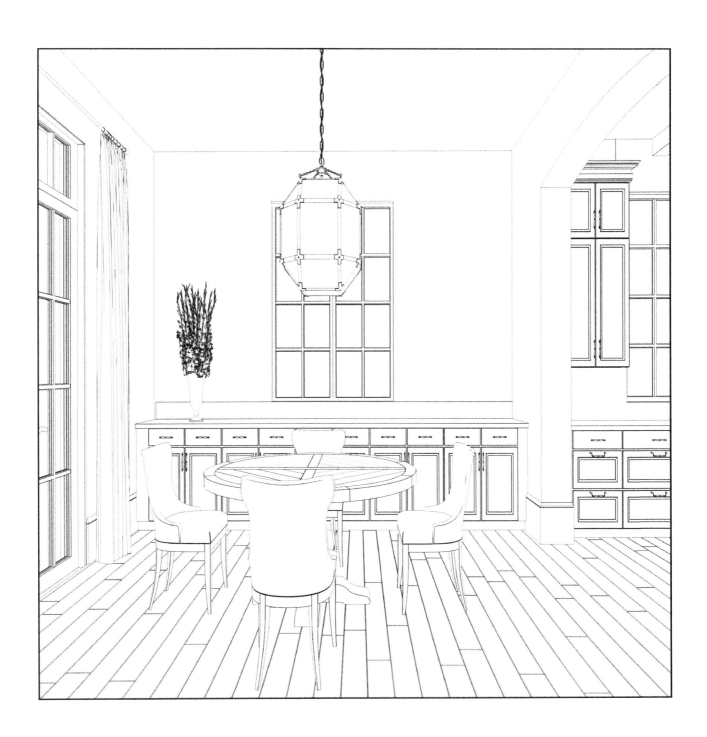

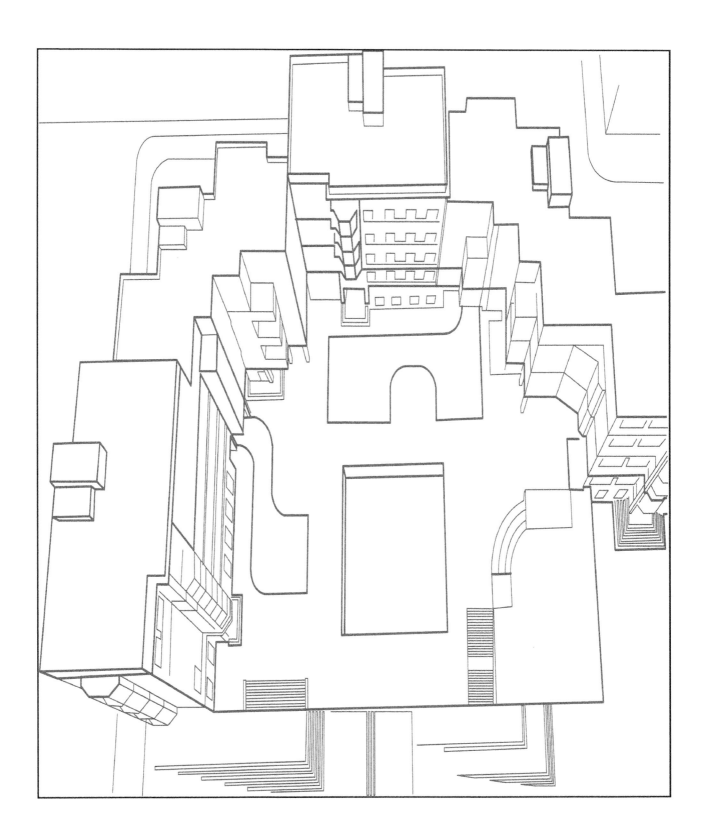

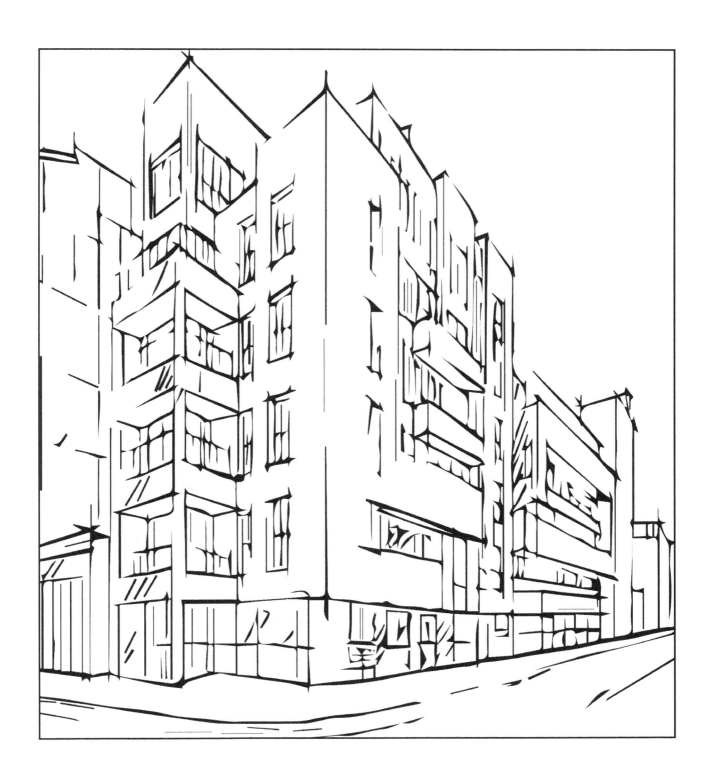

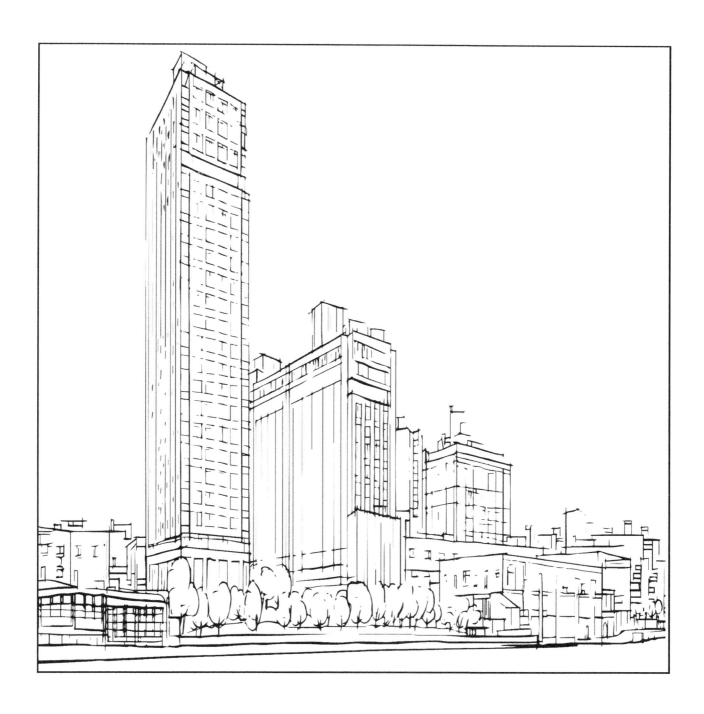

Made in the USA
Monee, IL
01 July 2020